YOUR FAMILY TREE

Exploring Immigration

by Jim Ollhoff

Visit us at
www.abdopublishing.com

Published by ABDO Publishing Company, 8000 West 78th Street, Suite 310, Edina, MN 55439. Copyright ©2011 by Abdo Consulting Group, Inc. International copyrights reserved in all countries. No part of this book may be reproduced in any form without written permission from the publisher. ABDO & Daughters™ is a trademark and logo of ABDO Publishing Company.

Printed in the United States of America, North Mankato, Minnesota
052010
092010

 PRINTED ON RECYCLED PAPER

Editor: John Hamilton
Graphic Design: Sue Hamilton
Cover Design: John Hamilton
Cover Photo: Getty Images
Interior Photos: Ancestry.com-pg 12; AP-pgs 16, 17, 20, 21, 24, 26 & 27; Church of Jesus Christ of Latter-Day Saints-FamilySearch.org-pg 27; Corbis-pgs 4 & 20; Getty Images-pgs 1 & 15; iStockphoto-pg 3; Granger Collection-pgs 5, 7, 13 & 22; Library of Congress-pgs 6, 8, 9, 14, 16, 18, 19, 23, 25, 28 & 32; North Wind Picture Archives-pg 11; Thinkstock-pgs 29 & 31.

Library of Congress Cataloging-in-Publication Data

Ollhoff, Jim, 1959-
  Exploring immigration / Jim Ollhoff.
    p. cm. -- (Your family tree)
  Includes index.
  ISBN 978-1-61613-463-1
  1. United States--Emigration and immigration--Juvenile literature. 2. Immigrants--United States--Juvenile literature. 3. United States--Genealogy--Juvenile literature. I. Title.
  JV6450.O45 2011
  304.8'73--dc22
                    2009050807

Contents

Coming to a New Country

The voyage was long and dangerous. The storms of the Atlantic Ocean threatened to turn the ship upside down. Food was scarce, and several people died along the way. Many wondered if the new land they were traveling to was really as wonderful as they had heard. Many people questioned whether they should have left the old country at all.

Below: An Italian woman newly arrived in America in the early 1900s.

Then, one morning, the passengers stood at the front of the ship. Off in the distance, they saw a large statue of a woman holding a torch. It was the Statue of Liberty. They had arrived in America at last.

If your ancestors came from Europe after 1886, then perhaps their first glimpse of America was the Statue of Liberty in New York City. For thousands of immigrants, the Statue of Liberty was the welcoming sign of their new country.

No matter where your ancestors came from, they found a home in America. There have always been many different groups in this country. North America has always been a rich mosaic of people from different lands and cultures.

Above: Immigrants who came from Europe after 1886 often saw the Statue of Liberty in New York Harbor, and knew they had arrived in America.

Why People Immigrate

People came to North America for many reasons. Usually, these reasons could be put into two categories. Some people were *pushed* out of their old countries, and others were *pulled* to the new country.

People were pushed out of a country when staying was just too painful, and they were forced to leave. For example, some people were forced to go because of drought or famine. If it didn't rain, the crops dried up, and people had no food. In the 17th and 18th centuries, people couldn't go to the grocery store to buy food. They had to rely on area farmers. Sometimes insects or fungus destroyed much of the harvest, creating severe food shortages.

People were also pushed out of their countries because of wars. As armies passed through villages, soldiers often took food and supplies for themselves. Sometimes war caused so much destruction that it was no longer possible to live near the battle zones. The military also often conscripted people. Citizens were kidnapped and forced to serve as soldiers.

Above: A young Russian immigrant arrives in America in 1905.

Poverty was another reason people were pushed out of their old countries. In many countries, jobs were lost, money was scarce, and land was extremely expensive. In Germany in the 1800s, for example, land had been subdivided and sold so often that many of the fields were too small to support a family's needs.

The other main reason for immigration was the "pull" of America. Land was cheap, and there was plenty of it. There was no military conscription or wars being fought in the countryside. The vast open range provided plenty of adventure for a family that wanted to start over.

Many American states actually took out advertisements or created booklets that could be distributed in other countries. The ads told about how each state was a wonderful place to live, and encouraged immigrants to settle there.

People also came to this country because of chain migration. Chain migration is when one family or family member comes here and settles down. Then they write letters to family and friends in the old country, telling them that this is a wonderful place, and that they should move here also. Those people then immigrate, and in turn send letters to even more friends and family, who also join them in North America.

Left: Migrant workers in California in the mid-1900s. Many people followed friends and family members to America.

Above: A Polish family picks berries on a farm near Baltimore, Maryland, in 1909. Many immigrants came to America looking for work and a better life.

The First Immigration to North America

The first people came to North America at least 12,000 years ago, and probably much earlier. These first settlers, sometimes called Paleo-Indians, probably became the ancestors of most of the Native American tribes. Historians still have many questions about how and when people first came here.

Above: Some historians believed that Asians crossed the Bering Strait about 12,000 years ago.

Traditionally, historians believed that Asians crossed the Bering Strait about 12,000 to 15,000 years ago. At this time, the water level of the oceans was lower because much of it was frozen in giant glaciers. People were able to walk from Asia to North America on dry land. They probably followed animal herds that they needed for food.

Recent scientific evidence hints that people were in North and South America even earlier than 15,000 years ago. They probably arrived by boat.

Above: Paleo-Indians may have followed animal herds to North America thousands of years ago. They likely became the ancestors of most of the Native American tribes.

By the time Christopher Columbus arrived on the islands of the Caribbean in 1492, most of North and South America was already populated. More than 500 languages were spoken by many tribes and Indian nations. The population estimates of North America in 1492 vary wildly. Some historians say there were one million Native Americans. Other historians say there were as many as 18 million. The population of South America was much higher.

If you have Native American ancestry, you might want to look at the United States Indian Census Schedules, 1885–1940. The schedules are the censuses of the Indian nations that lived on reservations and cooperated with the federal government. Many of these censuses were done annually, although the quality of the information varies. The schedules are held in the National Archives. Go to:

www.archives.gov

for more information, or ask a librarian for help. The schedules are also available online at Ancestry.com, a website that requires payment to view its holdings.

There is a huge amount of information about Native American genealogy online. If you know the tribal affiliations of your ancestors, that will be a key to even more helpful information.

Above: Christopher Columbus arrived on the islands of the Caribbean in 1492. The Italian explorer discovered the islands populated by many tribes and Indian nations.

European Immigration

In the first two centuries of immigration to the United States, the majority of the settlers were Europeans. Often leaving their country because of poverty or warfare, they sought a place that was free of war and had wide-open spaces for farming. Most of the immigrants became farmers, often working as hired hands until they could afford a farm of their own. From 1820 through the 1880s, about 15 million people came to this country looking for a new home.

When immigrants came to this country, they often settled with other people from their home countries. This produced small communities of people from Sweden, or Germany, or Norway. Within these communities, people could speak their native language and celebrate the holidays and customs of their original culture.

Above: A painting showing a young German couple planning their immigration to the United States.

Above: The Castle Garden immigration center in New York City.

Above: The Ellis Island immigration center opened in 1892.

Left: Some of the United States's largest groups of immigrants came from Germany.

Many European immigrants in the 1800s came through the Castle Garden immigration center in New York City. If you have ancestors who came through this center, you might find them listed at the Castle Garden immigration center website:

www.castlegarden.org

This free online database lists records of immigrants entering the country. In 1892, the United States opened Ellis Island as the new immigration center. You might find your ancestors listed at Ellis Island's free website:

www.ellisisland.org

Some of the largest groups of immigrants in the early years of the United States came from Great Britain and Germany. Today, about 40 million people in the United States identify Germany as the homeland of their ancestors.

Above: When the potato crops failed in Ireland in the 1800s, many Irish immigrants came to the United States.

Many Irish immigrants came to the United States during the years 1845–1849. This time was called the "Great Irish Potato Famine." The potato had become a staple of the Irish diet. People relied on potatoes to survive. Beginning in the 1840s, a disease destroyed the potato crop in Ireland, resulting in widespread hunger and starvation. During this time, about 1.5 million Irish people immigrated to the United States.

African Immigration

Below: A photo from 1862 showing five generations of African Americans who lived on a plantation in Beaufort, South Carolina. Some African American slaves took the last name of their slave owner. Some did not.

The 1870 United States census is important for African American genealogists. It was the first census taken after the Civil War, which ended in 1865. For the new census, African Americans who had been slaves were now listed by name. Before the 1870 census, slaves were only listed as tally marks.

It's possible that if your ancestors were in this country before the Civil War, they may have been slaves. However, don't assume that your ancestors were slaves. There were 200,000 free African Americans in the Northern states, and about that many in the Southern states. If your ancestor was a slave, you'll need to find out the name of the slave owner. It's possible that the slave took the last name of the slave owner. This becomes rather complicated, because you have to research the slave owner, and also the state laws governing slaves. You might find hints about where in Africa the slaves came from. In fact, you might find out that your ancestors lived in the Caribbean Islands or Canada after leaving Africa.

18

Above: An African American man reads an 1863 newspaper with information on the Emancipation Proclamation. Even before slavery was abolished, there were many free African Americans in the Northern and Southern states in the 1800s.

The horrors of slavery also make for a very difficult path tracing your ancestors. You'll need to study the history of slavery as well as the places your ancestors lived. You will run into a lot of brick walls when tracing the history of slaves. However, finding even small pieces of information can lead you further back toward your roots.

Left and Below: Alex Haley traced the story of his ancestor, Kunte Kinte, who was brought as a slave from Africa to America in 1767. Haley's 1976 novel, *Roots: The Saga of an American Family,* became a famous TV mini-series in 1977.

If your ancestors were recent immigrants from Africa, then you probably have relatives who can share stories with you. Many recent African immigrants have come from countries torn by war. For example, Somalia is a country on the east side of Africa. It has been ravaged by civil war for a long time. This has created a humanitarian disaster, with widespread homelessness and hunger. In recent years, many Somalians have been able to emigrate to other countries, including the United States.

Below: A Somalian woman is presented with her American naturalization certificate in St. Louis, Missouri.

Asian Immigration

Above: Chinese immigrants arrive in San Francisco, California. Many came to America in search of gold.

In 1849, word spread across the world that gold had been discovered in California. Wild rumors spread that gold was lying on the ground, waiting for people to pick it up. People from all over the world came to California, including a large group of Chinese immigrants. By 1851, about 25,000 Chinese immigrants had come to California.

Above: Japanese people gather for a celebration in 1916 on the island of Oahu, Hawaii. Many Japanese immigrants came to Hawaii and the West Coast of the United States in the 1870s. Prior to that time, very few Japanese people were allowed to leave their country.

Japanese immigrants started coming to Hawaii and the West Coast in the 1870s. Before 1868, Japan was closed to outsiders, and few Japanese people were allowed to leave. After 1868, in a time called the Meiji Restoration, Japan opened its borders and began to rapidly industrialize. Suddenly, foreign competitors put small Japanese companies out of business. With few other options, many Japanese people came to the United States in search of work. Like many immigrants, they often faced hostility and discrimination.

Jewish and Middle Eastern Immigration

Below: Inventor Luther Simjian came to America from Turkey in 1920. He created such famous devices as the teleprompter and the self-focusing camera.

People of Jewish ancestry began coming to the United States in the 1600s, and continued to immigrate in waves throughout the years, often to escape religious persecution. Unfortunately, many of them were met with hostility in the United States as well.

If you have Jewish ancestors, there are a number of associations dedicated to helping you. Like most ancestry groups, Jewish ancestries have discussion boards, books, and websites to connect you with your roots.

People from Middle Eastern lands also came to the United States. In the late 1800s and early 1900s, more than 200,000 immigrants came from the Ottoman Empire (modern-day Turkey). The number of Middle Eastern immigrants dropped after 1924, when a new United States law began to strictly control the number of non-European immigrants. The law was dropped in 1965.

Above: One of the most famous Jewish immigrants was the brilliant German-born scientist Albert Einstein. He fled Europe in 1933 because of the rise to power of Adolf Hitler and the Nazi Party. Einstein received his certificate of American citizenship in 1940.

Hispanic Immigration

Below: In 1848, thousands of Mexicans living in the Southwest became Americans.

Spanish-speaking people have always played a part in the history of the United States. Some of the first Europeans in North America were Spaniards. The Mexican people have a diverse ancestry, including Spanish and Native American cultures.

One of the largest Mexican emigrations happened in 1848, but it wasn't the people who moved, it was political boundaries. In 1846, a war broke out between Mexico and the United States. The United States won, and in 1848, Mexico gave up a large section of land. This land included today's states of California, Arizona, New Mexico, Nevada, and others. Suddenly, thousands of Mexican people lived in the United States. Mexican immigration continued at a high level, and continues to this day.

If you have Mexican ancestors, it's likely that there are records of them in Mexico. Church records have been kept since the 1500s, and civil records have been kept since the mid-1800s. You'll need to know the city or village where your ancestors lived. Most people in Mexico were Roman Catholic, and they were members of the nearest church. These churches had territories, called parishes. Everyone from the parish went to the same church. Many of these records are available for free at www.familysearch.org. If not, you may have to write a letter directly to the parish or local civil registry.

Above: Academy Award-winning actor Anthony Rudolph Oaxaca Quinn was born in Mexico in 1915. To escape the Mexican Revolution, Quinn was smuggled into Texas by his mother when he was less than a year old.

A Melting Pot or a Chunky Stew?

Above: If you have Irish relatives who came to America in the mid-1840s, it is likely they moved to escape the potato famine in Ireland.

As you write up the history of your family, you can learn about the history of lands from which your ancestors came. You can say, "Great-Great-Grandpa O'Malley came to this country in 1849. Since this was during the Irish potato famine, it's possible that he left because of the harsh conditions in Ireland."

Sometimes the United States has been called a "melting pot." This term refers to the idea that people of all cultures and lands have come to the United States, and have left their old ways to become Americans.

Perhaps a better way to describe American immigration is that the United States is a "chunky stew." Immigrants have usually not left their old ways. Instead, they have moved in with other people of the same culture, from the same lands. So, the United States is a collection of different groups of people, all with different ancestries and different backgrounds. This is a rich mosaic of peoples.

Above: People of all cultures and lands have come to live in the United States.

Glossary

ANCESTORS

The people from whom you are directly descended. Usually this refers to people in generations prior to your grandparents.

ANCESTRY.COM

A massive series of databases for genealogical research. It is a subscription site, which means you have to pay to use the site. Some libraries subscribe to the site, so you may be able to use it for free. Check with your local library.

BERING STRAIT

The small waterway that divides Siberia, a vast area of central and eastern Russia, from Alaska. It was discovered by Vitus Bering in 1728.

CENSUS

The government's records that show information about who lives in this country and where they live. Also the process of collecting that information.

CHAIN MIGRATION

A family settles in a new country. Then they write letters to family and friends in the old country, inviting them to come to the new country. Those people settle in the new country, and then send invitations to more friends and family in the old country.

EMIGRATION

The process of leaving one country to live in another. For example, *Jacob O'Malley emigrated from Ireland.*

FAMILYSEARCH.ORG

A free website run by the Church of Jesus Christ of Latter-Day Saints. It provides a huge database of genealogical materials.

GENEALOGY

The study of your ancestors and your family history.

IMMIGRATION

The process of entering a country in order to live there. For example, *Jacob O'Malley immigrated to the United States.*

MIGRATION

When a group of people moves from one place to another.

PALEO-INDIANS

Considered to be the first residents of North and South America, they came to the hemisphere at least 12,000 years ago, and probably much earlier. They are the ancestors of modern Native Americans.

STATUE OF LIBERTY

A 151-foot (46-m) -tall statue that stands on Liberty Island in New York Harbor. It was given to America by the people of France, and dedicated in 1886. It is a symbol of freedom for millions of immigrants who come to America.

Index

A Chinese-American family in California around 1900.